Bird Calm

Adult Coloring Book

Bird Calm

Adult Coloring Book

KF Wheatie & KM Wheatie

Strawberryhead &
Gingerbread Press

www.strawberryheadandgingerbread.com

Bird Calm

Published by Strawberryhead and Gingerbread Press
https://www.strawberryheadandgingerbread.com

Copyright © 2025 by KF Wheatie & KM Wheatie

All rights reserved. Neither this book, nor any parts within it may be sold or reproduced in any form or by any electronic or mechanical means, including information storage and retrieval systems, without permission in writing from the author. The only exception is by a reviewer, who may quote short excerpts in a review.

ISBN: 979-8-9986856-2-0 (paperback)

KF Wheatie, nicknamed Strawberryhead, was diagnosed with autism as a child. KF uses her strong faith to achieve many of life's endeavors. She is a 2024 college graduate with a B.A. in Fine Arts and Music Minor. KF makes it her mission to make new friends as she goes along her many journeys. Additionally, KF is a classically trained professional harpist. Her hobbies include art, Broadway, and travel.

KM Wheatie is nicknamed Gingerbread, was diagnosed with autism at an early age. KM preferred to play alone as a child. It was not that he did not want to interact with other kids; he did not have the social skills necessary to play with them. He turned his love of map reading into a dedicated hobby. He is a 2024 college graduate with a B.S. degree in Environmental Science (GIS) and Art Minor. His hobbies include riding rollercoasters, traveling, and hiking.

KF and KM want all children and adults, with or without a disability, to be encouraged when they encounter struggles of loneliness and hardship.

Visit KF & KM at their interactive web site:
StrawberryheadandGingerbread.com